PRACTICE
JAVASCRIPT

160 Solved Exercises to
Accelerate your Learning

PRACTICE JAVASCRIPT

160 Solved Exercises to Accelerate your Learning

Ruhan Avila da Conceição

1st edition
ISBN: 9798871977323

Independently published
Kindle Direct Publishing
Amazon Inc.

Summary

Copyright Notice

Preface

Welcome to this book where solved and commented Javascript exercises are presented. In this book, you will find a collection of 160 exercises designed to help you improve your programming skills in this powerful language.

Learning to program involves not only understanding theoretical concepts but also applying those concepts in real-life situations. That's exactly what you will find in this book: a wide variety of problems ranging from basic fundamentals to more complex challenges.

As you progress through the exercises, you will be challenged with tasks involving mathematical formula manipulation, strings, conditionals, loops, vector manipulation, matrices, and much more.

The main goal of this book is to provide a practical and comprehensive resource for programmers seeking improvement. Whether you are a beginner in Javascript looking to solidify your knowledge or an experienced programmer wishing to deepen your expertise, these exercises will serve as an excellent study guide and reference. This book is also suitable for teachers who would like to have a rich collection of solved Programming Logic exercises to create exercises and questions for their students.

Enjoy this learning journey and dive into the solved and commented Javascript exercises. Prepare yourself for stimulating challenges, creative solutions, and a unique opportunity to enhance your programming skills.

This book was written using artificial intelligence tools in content creation, but all materials have been reviewed and edited by the author to deliver a final high-quality product.

Happy reading, happy studying, and have fun exploring the fascinating world of Javascript programming

Ruhan Avila da Conceição.

Introduction

If you have acquired this book, you want to start programming and be logically challenged as soon as possible, without wanting to read a sermon on the mount. But it is important to highlight a few things before we begin.

Even though many exercises may be considered easy, if you are new to this programming journey, it is important for you to first try to solve the problem on your own before looking at the solution. There is more than one possible solution to the same problem, and you need to think and develop your own solution. Then, you can compare it with the proposed one in the book, identify the strengths of each, and try to learn a little more.

If the exercise is too difficult and you can't solve it, move on to the next one and try again the next day. Don't immediately jump to the answer, even if you can't solve it, and definitely don't look at the answer without even attempting to solve it.

Learning programming logic is not about getting the answer; it's about the journey you take to arrive at the answer.

With that being said, the remaining chapters of this book are divided according to the programming topics covered in the proposed exercises.

From now on, it's all up to you!

Basic Exercises

Before starting the exercises, it's important to carefully read this. When a particular exercise requires user input, the *prompt* command will be used. However, please note that the *prompt-sync* package needs to be installed beforehand. To do this, initiate an npm project and install the package using the following steps:

```
npm init
npm install prompt-sync
```

Additionally, you must add the following command in the first line in your code:

```
prompt = require("prompt-sync")()
```

1. Write a program that prints "Hello World!" on the screen.

```
console.log("Hello World!");
```

2. Write a program that prints "Hello" on one line and "World!" on the bottom line, using two different commands.

```
console.log("Hello");
console.log("World!");
```

3. Write a program that prints "Hello" on one line and "World!" on the bottom line, using only one command to print.

```
console.log("Hello\nWorld!");
```

4. Write a program that prints "Hello" on one line and "World!" on the bottom line, leaving a blank line between the words.

```
console.log("Hello");
console.log(""); // Blank line
console.log("World!");
```

5. Write a program that prints "Hello World!" (in the same line) on the screen, using one command to print "Hello" and another command to print "World!".

```
process.stdout.write("Hello ");
process.stdout.write("World!");
console.log(); // Add a newline to move to the next
line
```

To do this, you must run this command before: npm i --save-dev @types/node

6. Write a program that prints "Hello World!" (in the same line) on the screen, using one command to print "Hello", another command to print "World", and another to print "!".

```
process.stdout.write("Hello ");
process.stdout.write("World");
process.stdout.write("!");
console.log(); // Add a newline to move to the next
line
```

7. Make a program that asks for the user's name, and prints the name on the screen immediately after.

```
// This command below will be omitted in next exercises
prompt = require("prompt-sync")()

const userName = prompt("Please enter your name:");
```

```
console.log("Hello, " + userName + "!");
```

8. Make a program that reads the names of three people in sequence, followed by their respective ages, and prints each name with their respective ages on the screen.

```
// Read information for the first person
const name1 = prompt("Enter the name of the first
person:");
const age1 = prompt("Enter the age of the first
person:");

// Read information for the second person
const name2 = prompt("Enter the name of the second
person:");
const age2 = prompt("Enter the age of the second
person:");

// Read information for the third person
const name3 = prompt("Enter the name of the third
person:");
const age3 = prompt("Enter the age of the third
person:");

// Print each person's name and age
console.log(name1 + " is " + age1 + " years old.");
console.log(name2 + " is " + age2 + " years old.");
console.log(name3 + " is " + age3 + " years old.");
```

9. Make a program that reads the names of three people in sequence, followed by their respective ages and heights, and prints the data in table format on the screen.

```
// Read information for the first person
const name1 = prompt("Enter the name of the first
```

```
person:");
const age1 = prompt("Enter the age of the first
person:");
const height1 = prompt("Enter the height of the first
person (in cm):");

// Read information for the second person
const name2 = prompt("Enter the name of the second
person:");
const age2 = prompt("Enter the age of the second
person:");
const height2 = prompt("Enter the height of the second
person (in cm):");

// Read information for the third person
const name3 = prompt("Enter the name of the third
person:");
const age3 = prompt("Enter the age of the third
person:");
const height3 = prompt("Enter the height of the third
person (in cm):");

// Print the data in table format
console.log("Name\tAge\tHeight (cm)");
console.log(name1 + "\t" + age1 + "\t" + height1);
console.log(name2 + "\t" + age2 + "\t" + height2);
console.log(name3 + "\t" + age3 + "\t" + height3);
```

10. Make a program that reads the names of three people in sequence, followed by reading their respective ages and heights, and prints the data on the screen in table format, using dashes (-) to separate rows and pipes (|) to separate columns.

```
// Read information for the first person
const name1 = prompt("Enter the name of the first
person:");
const age1 = prompt("Enter the age of the first
```

```javascript
person:");
const height1 = prompt("Enter the height of the first
person (in cm):");

// Read information for the second person
const name2 = prompt("Enter the name of the second
person:");
const age2 = prompt("Enter the age of the second
person:");
const height2 = prompt("Enter the height of the second
person (in cm):");

// Read information for the third person
const name3 = prompt("Enter the name of the third
person:");
const age3 = prompt("Enter the age of the third
person:");
const height3 = prompt("Enter the height of the third
person (in cm):");

// Print the data in table format with dashes and pipes
console.log("Name\t| Age\t| Height (cm)");
console.log("---------------------------------");
console.log(name1 + "\t| " + age1 + "\t| " + height1);
console.log(name2 + "\t| " + age2 + "\t| " + height2);
console.log(name3 + "\t| " + age3 + "\t| " + height3);
```

Mathematical Formulas

11. Write a program that prompts the user for two numbers and displays the addition, subtraction, multiplication, and division between them.

```
// Prompt the user for the first number
const firstNumber = parseFloat(prompt("Enter the first
number:"));

// Prompt the user for the second number
const secondNumber = parseFloat(prompt("Enter the
second number:"));

// Perform the calculations and display the results
const addition = firstNumber + secondNumber;
const subtraction = firstNumber - secondNumber;
const multiplication = firstNumber * secondNumber;
const division = firstNumber / secondNumber;

console.log("Addition: " + addition);
console.log("Subtraction: " + subtraction);
console.log("Multiplication: " + multiplication);
console.log("Division: " + division);
```

12. Write a program that calculates the arithmetic mean of two numbers entered by the user.

```
// Prompt the user for the first number
const firstNumber = parseFloat(prompt("Enter the first
number:"));

// Prompt the user for the second number
const secondNumber = parseFloat(prompt("Enter the
second number:"));

// Calculate the arithmetic mean
```

```javascript
const mean = (firstNumber + secondNumber) / 2;

// Display the result
console.log("The arithmetic mean of " + firstNumber + "
and " + secondNumber + " is: " + mean);
```

13. Create a program that calculates and displays the arithmetic mean of three numbers entered by the user.

```javascript
// Prompt the user for the first number
const firstNumber = parseFloat(prompt("Enter the first
number:"));

// Prompt the user for the second number
const secondNumber = parseFloat(prompt("Enter the
second number:"));

// Prompt the user for the third number
const thirdNumber = parseFloat(prompt("Enter the third
number:"));

// Calculate the arithmetic mean
const mean = (firstNumber + secondNumber + thirdNumber)
/ 3;

// Display the result
console.log(
  "The arithmetic mean of " +
    firstNumber +
    ", " +
    secondNumber +
    ", and " +
    thirdNumber +
    " is: " +
    mean
);
```

14. Write a program that reads two numbers, the first being the base and the second the exponent, and then printing the first number raised to the second.

```
// Prompt the user for the base number
const base = parseFloat(prompt("Enter the base
number:"));

// Prompt the user for the exponent
const exponent = parseFloat(prompt("Enter the
exponent:"));

// Calculate the result using the Math.pow() function
const result = Math.pow(base, exponent);

// Display the result
console.log(base + " raised to the power of " +
exponent + " is: " + result);
```

15. Write a program that reads a number and prints the square root of the number on the screen.

```
// Prompt the user for a number
const userInput = parseFloat(prompt("Enter a
number:"));

// Calculate the square root regardless of whether the
input is valid
const squareRoot = Math.sqrt(userInput);

// Display the result
console.log("The square root of " + userInput + " is: "
+ squareRoot);
```

16. Write a program that calculates the geometric mean of three numbers entered by the user →

$$GeoMean = \sqrt[3]{n_1 \times n_2 \times n_3}$$

```javascript
// Prompt the user for the first number
const number1 = parseFloat(prompt("Enter the first
number:"));

// Prompt the user for the second number
const number2 = parseFloat(prompt("Enter the second
number:"));

// Prompt the user for the third number
const number3 = parseFloat(prompt("Enter the third
number:"));

// Calculate the geometric mean regardless of the input
values
const geometricMean = Math.pow(number1 * number2 *
number3, 1 / 3);

// Display the result
console.log("The geometric mean of " + number1 + ", " +
number2 + ", and " + number3 + " is: " +
geometricMean);
```

17. Write a program that calculates the BMI of an individual, using the formula BMI = weight / height²

```javascript
// Prompt the user for their weight in kilograms
const weight = parseFloat(prompt("Enter your weight in
kilograms:"));

// Prompt the user for their height in meters
const height = parseFloat(prompt("Enter your height in
meters:"));

// Calculate the BMI
```

```javascript
const bmi = weight / (height * height);

// Display the BMI
console.log("Your Body Mass Index (BMI) is: " +
bmi.toFixed(2));
```

18. Create a program that calculates and displays the perimeter of a circle, prompting the user for the radius, using the formula P = 2πr

```javascript
// Prompt the user for the radius of the circle
const radius = parseFloat(prompt("Enter the radius of
the circle:"));

// Calculate the perimeter (circumference) regardless
of the input value
const perimeter = 2 * Math.PI * radius;

// Display the perimeter
console.log("The perimeter (circumference) of the
circle is: " + perimeter.toFixed(2));
```

19. Write a program that calculates the area of a circle from the radius, using the formula A = πr²

```javascript
// Prompt the user for the radius of the circle
const radius = parseFloat(prompt("Enter the radius of
the circle:"));

// Calculate the area of the circle
const area = Math.PI * Math.pow(radius, 2);

// Display the area
console.log("The area of the circle is: " +
area.toFixed(2));
```

20. Write a program that calculates the delta of a quadratic equation (Δ = b² - 4ac).

```
// Prompt the user for the coefficients a, b, and c of
the quadratic equation
const a = parseFloat(prompt("Enter the coefficient
a:"));
const b = parseFloat(prompt("Enter the coefficient
b:"));
const c = parseFloat(prompt("Enter the coefficient
c:"));

// Calculate the delta without using if statements
const delta = b * b - 4 * a * c;

// Display the delta
console.log("The delta (Δ) of the quadratic equation
is: " + delta);
```

21. Write a program that calculates the perimeter and area of a rectangle, using the formulas P = 2(w + l) and A = wl, where w is the width and l is the length

```
// Prompt the user for the width and length of the
rectangle
const width = parseFloat(prompt("Enter the width of the
rectangle:"));
const length = parseFloat(prompt("Enter the length of
the rectangle:"));

// Calculate the perimeter and area of the rectangle
const perimeter = 2 * (width + length);
const area = width * length;

// Display the results
console.log("The perimeter of the rectangle is: " +
perimeter);
console.log("The area of the rectangle is: " + area);
```

22. Write a program that calculates the perimeter and area of a triangle, using the formulas P = a + b + c and A = (b * h) / 2, where a, b and c are the sides of the triangle and h is the height relative to the side B.

```javascript
// Prompt the user for the lengths of the triangle's
three sides
const sideA = parseFloat(prompt("Enter the length of
side A:"));
const sideB = parseFloat(prompt("Enter the length of
side B:"));
const sideC = parseFloat(prompt("Enter the length of
side C:"));

// Prompt the user for the height relative to side B
const heightToSideB = parseFloat(prompt("Enter the
height relative to side B:"));

// Calculate the perimeter of the triangle
const perimeter = sideA + sideB + sideC;

// Calculate the area of the triangle
const area = (sideB * heightToSideB) / 2;

// Display the results
console.log("The perimeter of the triangle is: " +
perimeter);
console.log("The area of the triangle is: " + area);
```

23. Write a program that calculates the average velocity of an object, using the formula v = Δs/Δt, where v is the average velocity, Δs is the space variation, and Δt is the time variation

```javascript
// Prompt the user for the space variation (Δs) in
meters
const spaceVariation = parseFloat(prompt("Enter the
space variation (Δs) in meters:"));
```

```javascript
// Prompt the user for the time variation (Δt) in
seconds
const timeVariation = parseFloat(prompt("Enter the time
variation (Δt) in seconds:"));

// Calculate the average velocity
const averageVelocity = spaceVariation / timeVariation;

// Display the result
console.log("The average velocity of the object is: " +
averageVelocity.toFixed(2) + " m/s");
```

24. Write a program that calculates the kinetic energy of a moving object, using the formula E = (mv²) / 2, where E is the kinetic energy, m is the mass of the object, and v is the velocity.

```javascript
// Prompt the user for the mass of the object in
kilograms
const mass = parseFloat(prompt("Enter the mass of the
object (in kilograms):"));

// Prompt the user for the velocity of the object in
meters per second
const velocity = parseFloat(prompt("Enter the velocity
of the object (in meters per second):"));

// Calculate the kinetic energy
const kineticEnergy = (mass * Math.pow(velocity, 2)) /
2;

// Display the result
console.log("The kinetic energy of the object is: " +
kineticEnergy.toFixed(2) + " joules");
```

25. Write a program that calculates the work done by a force acting on an object, using the formula W = F * d, where W is the work, F is the applied force, and d is the distance traveled by the object.

```
// Prompt the user for the applied force in newtons
const force = parseFloat(prompt("Enter the applied
force (in newtons):"));

// Prompt the user for the distance traveled by the
object in meters
const distance = parseFloat(prompt("Enter the distance
traveled by the object (in meters):"));

// Calculate the work done
const work = force * distance;

// Display the result
console.log("The work done by the force is: " +
work.toFixed(2) + " joules");
```

26. Write a program that calculates the n-th term of an arithmetic progression given the value of the first term, the common difference (ratio), and the value of n read from the user → $a_n = a_1 + (n - 1) \times r$

```
// Prompt the user for the first term (a)
const firstTerm = parseFloat(prompt("Enter the first
term (a) of the arithmetic progression:"));

// Prompt the user for the common difference (d)
const commonDifference = parseFloat(prompt("Enter the
common difference (d):"));

// Prompt the user for the value of n
const n = parseInt(prompt("Enter the value of n:"));

// Calculate the n-th term of the arithmetic
```

```
progression
const nthTerm = firstTerm + (n - 1) * commonDifference;

// Display the result
console.log("The " + n + "-th term of the arithmetic
progression is: " + nthTerm);
```

27. Write a program that reads the *x* and *y* position of two points in the Cartesian plane, and calculates the distance between them

```
// Prompt the user for the x and y coordinates of the
first point
const x1 = parseFloat(prompt("Enter the x-coordinate of
the first point:"));
const y1 = parseFloat(prompt("Enter the y-coordinate of
the first point:"));

// Prompt the user for the x and y coordinates of the
second point
const x2 = parseFloat(prompt("Enter the x-coordinate of
the second point:"));
const y2 = parseFloat(prompt("Enter the y-coordinate of
the second point:"));

// Calculate the distance between the two points
const distance = Math.sqrt(Math.pow(x2 - x1, 2) +
Math.pow(y2 - y1, 2));

// Display the result
console.log("The distance between the two points is: "
+ distance.toFixed(2));
```

28. Create a program that prompts the user for the radius of a sphere and calculates and displays its volume.

```
// Prompt the user for the radius of the sphere
const radius = parseFloat(prompt("Enter the radius of
the sphere:"));

// Calculate the volume of the sphere
const volume = (4/3) * Math.PI * Math.pow(radius, 3);

// Display the result
console.log("The volume of the sphere is: " +
volume.toFixed(2));
```

29. Make a program that reads the resistance of two resistors and displays the resulting resistance value when connected in series, adding the values, and in parallel using the formula (R1 * R2) / (R1 + R2)

```
// Prompt the user for the resistance value of the
first resistor (R1)
const resistance1 = parseFloat(prompt("Enter the
resistance value of the first resistor (R1):"));

// Prompt the user for the resistance value of the
second resistor (R2)
const resistance2 = parseFloat(prompt("Enter the
resistance value of the second resistor (R2):"));

// Calculate the equivalent resistance in series
const seriesResistance = resistance1 + resistance2;

// Calculate the equivalent resistance in parallel
const parallelResistance = (resistance1 * resistance2)
/ (resistance1 + resistance2);

// Display the results
```

```
console.log("Equivalent resistance in series: " +
seriesResistance.toFixed(2) + " ohms");
console.log("Equivalent resistance in parallel: " +
parallelResistance.toFixed(2) + " ohms");
```

30. Make a program that reads a value of a product and the tax (in percentage), and calculates the final value of it.

```
// Prompt the user for the initial value of the product
const initialValue = parseFloat(prompt("Enter the
initial value of the product:"));

// Prompt the user for the tax rate in percentage
const taxRate = parseFloat(prompt("Enter the tax rate
(in percentage):"));

// Calculate the final value of the product including
tax
const taxAmount = (initialValue * taxRate) / 100;
const finalValue = initialValue + taxAmount;

// Display the results
console.log("Tax Amount: $" + taxAmount.toFixed(2));
console.log("Final Value (including tax): $" +
finalValue.toFixed(2));
```

Conditionals

31. Make a program that asks for a person's age and displays whether they are of legal age or not (age >= 18).

```
// Prompt the user for their age
const age = parseInt(prompt("Please enter your age:"));

// Check if the age is greater than or equal to 18
const isLegalAge = age >= 18;

// Display the result
if (isLegalAge) {
  console.log("You are of legal age.");
} else {
  console.log("You are not of legal age.");
}
```

32. Write a program that reads a number and reports whether it is odd or even.

```
// Prompt the user for a number
const number = parseInt(prompt("Enter a number:"));

// Check if the number is odd or even
if (number % 2 === 0) {
  console.log(number + " is an even number.");
} else {
  console.log(number + " is an odd number.");
}
```

33. Write a program that reads a number and reports whether it is positive, negative or zero.

```
// Prompt the user for a number
```

```javascript
const number = parseFloat(prompt("Enter a number:"));

// Check whether the number is positive, negative, or
zero
if (number > 0) {
  console.log(number + " is a positive number.");
} else if (number < 0) {
  console.log(number + " is a negative number.");
} else {
  console.log(number + " is zero.");
}
```

34. Create a program that reads three numbers and checks if their sum is positive, negative or equal to zero

```javascript
// Prompt the user for three numbers
const number1 = parseFloat(prompt("Enter the first
number:"));
const number2 = parseFloat(prompt("Enter the second
number:"));
const number3 = parseFloat(prompt("Enter the third
number:"));

// Calculate the sum of the three numbers
const sum = number1 + number2 + number3;

// Check whether the sum is positive, negative, or zero
if (sum > 0) {
  console.log("The sum of the three numbers is
positive.");
} else if (sum < 0) {
  console.log("The sum of the three numbers is
negative.");
} else {
  console.log("The sum of the three numbers is zero.");
}
```

35. Write a program that reads two numbers and tells you which one is bigger.

```
// Prompt the user for the first number
const number1 = parseFloat(prompt("Enter the first
number:"));

// Prompt the user for the second number
const number2 = parseFloat(prompt("Enter the second
number:"));

// Compare the two numbers and find the bigger one
using an if statement
if (number1 > number2) {
  console.log(number1 + " is bigger than " + number2);
} else if (number2 > number1) {
  console.log(number2 + " is bigger than " + number1);
} else {
  console.log("Both numbers are equal.");
}
```

Without using if statement

```
// Prompt the user for the first number
const number1 = parseFloat(prompt("Enter the first
number:"));

// Prompt the user for the second number
const number2 = parseFloat(prompt("Enter the second
number:"));

// Find the bigger number using the Math.max function
const biggerNumber = Math.max(number1, number2);

// Display the result
console.log(biggerNumber + " is the bigger number.");
```

36. Write a program that asks the user for three numbers and displays the largest one.

```
// Prompt the user for three numbers
const number1 = parseFloat(prompt("Enter the first
number:"));
const number2 = parseFloat(prompt("Enter the second
number:"));
const number3 = parseFloat(prompt("Enter the third
number:"));

let largestNumber;

// Compare the numbers using if statements to find the
largest one
if (number1 >= number2 && number1 >= number3) {
  largestNumber = number1;
} else if (number2 >= number1 && number2 >= number3) {
  largestNumber = number2;
} else {
  largestNumber = number3;
}

// Display the largest number
console.log("The largest number is: " + largestNumber);
```

37. Make a program that reads three numbers, and informs if their sum is divisible by 5 or not.

```
// Prompt the user for three numbers
const number1 = parseInt(prompt("Enter the first
number:"));
const number2 = parseInt(prompt("Enter the second
number:"));
const number3 = parseInt(prompt("Enter the third
number:"));

// Calculate the sum of the three numbers
```

```
const sum = number1 + number2 + number3;

// Check if the sum is divisible by 5
if (sum % 5 === 0) {
  console.log("The sum of the three numbers (" + sum +
") is divisible by 5.");
} else {
  console.log("The sum of the three numbers (" + sum +
") is not divisible by 5.");
}
```

38. Write a program that asks for an integer and checks if it is divisible by 3 and 5 at the same time.

```
// Prompt the user for an integer
const number = parseInt(prompt("Enter an integer:"));

// Check if the number is divisible by both 3 and 5
if (number % 3 === 0 && number % 5 === 0) {
  console.log(number + " is divisible by both 3 and 5
at the same time.");
} else {
  console.log(number + " is not divisible by both 3 and
5 at the same time.");
}
```

39. Make a program that asks for two numbers and displays if the first is divisible by the second

```
// Prompt the user for two numbers
const number1 = parseInt(prompt("Enter the first
number:"));
const number2 = parseInt(prompt("Enter the second
number:"));

// Check if the first number is divisible by the second
number
```

```javascript
if (number2 !== 0 && number1 % number2 === 0) {
  console.log(number1 + " is divisible by " + number2);
} else {
  console.log(number1 + " is not divisible by " +
number2);
}
```

40. Make a program that reads the scores of two tests and reports whether the student passed (score greater than or equal to 6) or failed (score less than 6) in each of the tests.

```javascript
// Prompt the user for the scores of two tests
const test1Score = parseFloat(prompt("Enter the score
for test 1:"));
const test2Score = parseFloat(prompt("Enter the score
for test 2:"));

// Check if the student passed or failed in each test
if (test1Score >= 6) {
  console.log("Student passed test 1.");
} else {
  console.log("Student failed test 1.");
}

if (test2Score >= 6) {
  console.log("Student passed test 2.");
} else {
  console.log("Student failed test 2.");
}
```

41. Make a program that reads the grades of two tests, calculates the simple arithmetic mean, and informs whether the student passed (average greater than or equal to 6) or failed (average less than 6).

```javascript
// Prompt the user for the grades of two tests
```

```javascript
const test1Grade = parseFloat(prompt("Enter the grade
for test 1:"));
const test2Grade = parseFloat(prompt("Enter the grade
for test 2:"));

// Calculate the simple arithmetic mean
const average = (test1Grade + test2Grade) / 2;

// Check if the student passed or failed based on the
average
if (average >= 6) {
  console.log("Student passed. Average grade: " +
average.toFixed(2));
} else {
  console.log("Student failed. Average grade: " +
average.toFixed(2));
}
```

42. Make a program that reads the age of three people and how many of them are of legal age (age 18 or older).

```javascript
// Prompt the user for the age of three people
const age1 = parseInt(prompt("Enter the age of person
1:"));
const age2 = parseInt(prompt("Enter the age of person
2:"));
const age3 = parseInt(prompt("Enter the age of person
3:"));

// Count how many people are of legal age (18 or older)
let legalAgeCount = 0;

if (age1 >= 18) {
  legalAgeCount++;
}

if (age2 >= 18) {
```

```javascript
    legalAgeCount++;
}

if (age3 >= 18) {
  legalAgeCount++;
}

// Display the count of people who are of legal age
console.log("Number of people of legal age: " +
legalAgeCount);
```

43. Make a program that reads three numbers, and displays them on the screen in ascending order.

```javascript
// Prompt the user for three numbers
const number1 = parseFloat(prompt("Enter the first
number:"));
const number2 = parseFloat(prompt("Enter the second
number:"));
const number3 = parseFloat(prompt("Enter the third
number:"));

// Find the smallest, middle, and largest numbers
let smallest, middle, largest;

if (number1 <= number2 && number1 <= number3) {
  smallest = number1;
  if (number2 <= number3) {
    middle = number2;
    largest = number3;
  } else {
    middle = number3;
    largest = number2;
  }
} else if (number2 <= number1 && number2 <= number3) {
  smallest = number2;
  if (number1 <= number3) {
    middle = number1;
```

```
      largest = number3;
    } else {
      middle = number3;
      largest = number1;
    }
  } else {
    smallest = number3;
    if (number1 <= number2) {
      middle = number1;
      largest = number2;
    } else {
      middle = number2;
      largest = number1;
    }
  }
}

// Display the numbers in ascending order
console.log("Numbers in ascending order: " + smallest +
", " + middle + ", " + largest);
```

44. Write a program that reads three numbers and tells you if they can be the sides of a triangle (the sum of two sides must always be greater than the third side).

```
// Prompt the user for three numbers
const side1 = parseFloat(prompt("Enter the length of
side 1:"));
const side2 = parseFloat(prompt("Enter the length of
side 2:"));
const side3 = parseFloat(prompt("Enter the length of
side 3:"));

// Check if the numbers can form a triangle
const canFormTriangle = (side1 + side2 > side3) &&
(side2 + side3 > side1) && (side1 + side3 > side2);

// Display the result
if (canFormTriangle) {
```

```
  console.log("These numbers can form the sides of a
triangle.");
} else {
  console.log("These numbers cannot form a triangle.");
}
```

45. Make a program that reads the year of birth of a person and informs if he is able to vote (age greater than or equal to 16 years old).

```
// Prompt the user for the year of birth
const yearOfBirth = parseInt(prompt("Enter the year of
birth:"));

// Calculate the current year
const currentYear = new Date().getFullYear();

// Calculate the age
const age = currentYear - yearOfBirth;

// Check if the person is eligible to vote (age greater
than or equal to 16)
if (age >= 16) {
  console.log("You are eligible to vote.");
} else {
  console.log("You are not eligible to vote yet.");
}
```

46. Create a program that asks for a person's age and displays whether they are a child (0-12 years old), teenager (13-17 years old), adult (18-59 years old), or elderly (60 years old or older), using nested conditionals, without using logical operators.

```
// Prompt the user for their age
const age = parseInt(prompt("Enter your age:"));
```

```javascript
// Check the age range using nested if statements
if (age >= 0) {
  if (age <= 12) {
    console.log("You are a child.");
  } else if (age <= 17) {
    console.log("You are a teenager.");
  } else if (age <= 59) {
    console.log("You are an adult.");
  } else {
    console.log("You are elderly.");
  }
} else {
  console.log("Invalid age entered.");
}
```

47. Create a program that asks for a person's age and displays whether they are a child (0-12 years old), teenager (13-17 years old), adult (18-59 years old), or elderly (60 years old or older), using logical operators, without using else, elif, etc.

```javascript
// Prompt the user for their age
const age = parseInt(prompt("Enter your age:"));

// Check the age range using logical operators
const isChild = age >= 0 && age <= 12;
const isTeenager = age >= 13 && age <= 17;
const isAdult = age >= 18 && age <= 59;
const isElderly = age >= 60;

// Display the corresponding message based on the age
category
console.log(
  isChild ? "You are a child." :
  isTeenager ? "You are a teenager." :
  isAdult ? "You are an adult." :
  isElderly ? "You are elderly." :
  "Invalid age entered."
```

```
);
```

48. Make a program that reads a person's age and informs if he is not able to vote (age less than 16 years old), if he is able to vote but is not obligated (16, 17 years old, or age equal to or greater than 70 years), or if it is obligatory (18 to 69 years old).

```
// Prompt the user for their age
const age = parseInt(prompt("Enter your age:"));

// Check the age range and voting status
if (age < 16) {
  console.log("You are not able to vote.");
} else if (age >= 16 && age <= 17 || age >= 70) {
  console.log("You are able to vote but not
obligated.");
} else if (age >= 18 && age <= 69) {
  console.log("You are obligated to vote.");
} else {
  console.log("Invalid age entered.");
}
```

49. Make a program that reads three grades from a student and reports whether he passed (final grade greater than or equal to 7), failed (final grade less than 4) or was in recovery (final grade between 4 and 7).

```
// Prompt the user for three grades
const grade1 = parseFloat(prompt("Enter the first
grade:"));
const grade2 = parseFloat(prompt("Enter the second
grade:"));
const grade3 = parseFloat(prompt("Enter the third
grade:"));

// Calculate the average grade
```

```javascript
const averageGrade = (grade1 + grade2 + grade3) / 3;

// Report the student's status based on the final grade
if (averageGrade >= 7) {
  console.log("Student passed.");
} else if (averageGrade < 4) {
  console.log("Student failed.");
} else {
  console.log("Student is in recovery.");
}
```

50. Write a program that asks for a person's height and weight and calculates their body mass index (BMI), displaying the corresponding category (underweight, normal weight, overweight, obese, severely obese).

```javascript
// Prompt the user for their height in meters
const height = parseFloat(prompt("Enter your height in
meters:"));

// Prompt the user for their weight in kilograms
const weight = parseFloat(prompt("Enter your weight in
kilograms:"));

// Calculate the BMI
const bmi = weight / (height * height);

// Determine the BMI category
let category;
if (bmi < 18.5) {
  category = "Underweight";
} else if (bmi < 24.9) {
  category = "Normal weight";
} else if (bmi < 29.9) {
  category = "Overweight";
} else if (bmi < 34.9) {
  category = "Obese";
} else {
```

```
    category = "Severely obese";
}

// Display the BMI and corresponding category
console.log(`Your BMI is: ${bmi.toFixed(2)} -
${category}`);
```

51. Write a program that asks the user to enter their grade (0-100) and prints their letter grade (A for 90-100, B for 80-89, C for 70-79, D for 60-69, F for under 60).

```
// Prompt the user to enter their grade
const grade = parseInt(prompt("Enter your grade
(0-100):"));

// Determine the letter grade based on the entered
grade
let letterGrade;
if (grade >= 90 && grade <= 100) {
  letterGrade = 'A';
} else if (grade >= 80 && grade <= 89) {
  letterGrade = 'B';
} else if (grade >= 70 && grade <= 79) {
  letterGrade = 'C';
} else if (grade >= 60 && grade <= 69) {
  letterGrade = 'D';
} else {
  letterGrade = 'F';
}

// Display the corresponding letter grade
console.log(`Your letter grade is: ${letterGrade}`);
```

52. Write a program that reads the values *a*, *b* and *c* of a quadratic equation, and says if the roots of the function are real or imaginary.

```
// Prompt the user for coefficients of the quadratic
equation
const a = parseFloat(prompt("Enter the coefficient
a:"));
const b = parseFloat(prompt("Enter the coefficient
b:"));
const c = parseFloat(prompt("Enter the coefficient
c:"));

// Calculate the discriminant
const discriminant = b * b - 4 * a * c;

// Determine if roots are real or imaginary based on
the discriminant
if (discriminant > 0) {
  console.log("The roots of the quadratic equation are
real.");
} else if (discriminant === 0) {
  console.log("The roots of the quadratic equation are
real and equal.");
} else {
  console.log("The roots of the quadratic equation are
imaginary.");
}
```

53. Create a program that reads the price of a product. If the price is more than US$200, the tax is 5%, if it is more than US$500, the tax is 7.5%. Products up to US$200 do not pay taxes. Print the final price of the product on the screen.

```
// Prompt the user for the price of the product
const price = parseFloat(prompt("Enter the price of the
product:"));
```

```javascript
let finalPrice;

// Calculate the final price based on different tax
rates
if (price > 500) {
  finalPrice = price * 1.075; // 7.5% tax
} else if (price > 200) {
  finalPrice = price * 1.05; // 5% tax
} else {
  finalPrice = price; // No tax for products up to $200
}

// Display the final price of the product
console.log(`The final price of the product is:
$${finalPrice.toFixed(2)}`);
```

54. Write a program that reads a year (a four digit number) and checks whether it is a leap year or not.

```javascript
// Prompt the user for a four-digit year
const year = parseInt(prompt("Enter a four-digit
year:"));

let isLeapYear = false;

// Check if the year is a leap year
if ((year % 4 === 0 && year % 100 !== 0) || year % 400
=== 0) {
  isLeapYear = true;
}

// Display the result
if (isLeapYear) {
  console.log(`${year} is a leap year.`);
} else {
  console.log(`${year} is not a leap year.`);
}
```

55. Input three numbers representing the coefficients of a quadratic equation (a, b, c) and find its roots, also mention if they are real or complex

```javascript
// Prompt the user for coefficients of the quadratic
equation
const a = parseFloat(prompt("Enter the coefficient
a:"));
const b = parseFloat(prompt("Enter the coefficient
b:"));
const c = parseFloat(prompt("Enter the coefficient
c:"));

// Calculate the discriminant
const discriminant = b * b - 4 * a * c;

let root1, root2;
let rootsType;

// Calculate roots based on the discriminant
if (discriminant > 0) {
  rootsType = "Real and distinct";
  root1 = (-b + Math.sqrt(discriminant)) / (2 * a);
  root2 = (-b - Math.sqrt(discriminant)) / (2 * a);
} else if (discriminant === 0) {
  rootsType = "Real and equal";
  root1 = root2 = -b / (2 * a);
} else {
  rootsType = "Complex";
  const realPart = -b / (2 * a);
  const imaginaryPart =
Math.sqrt(Math.abs(discriminant)) / (2 * a);
  root1 = `${realPart.toFixed(2)} +
${imaginaryPart.toFixed(2)}i`;
  root2 = `${realPart.toFixed(2)} -
${imaginaryPart.toFixed(2)}i`;
}

// Display the roots and their nature
```

```
console.log(`Roots of the quadratic equation are:
${root1} and ${root2}`);
console.log(`Nature of roots: ${rootsType}`);
```

Repeat Loops

56. Write a program that displays the numbers 1 through 10 using a while loop.

```
let number = 1;

while (number <= 10) {
  console.log(number);
  number++;
}
```

57. Write a program that displays the numbers 1 through 10 using a for loop.

```
for (let number = 1; number <= 10; number++) {
  console.log(number);
}
```

58. Write a program that displays all numbers from 1 to 100, using a while loop.

```
let number = 1;

while (number <= 100) {
  console.log(number);
  number++;
}
```

59. Write a program that displays all numbers from 1 to 100, using a for loop.

```
for (let number = 1; number <= 100; number++) {
  console.log(number);
}
```

60. Write a program that displays all numbers from 1 to 100, using a do-while loop.

```
let number = 1;

do {
  console.log(number);
  number++;
} while (number <= 100);
```

61. Write a program that prints all even numbers from 1 to 100 using a while loop and an if statement inside the loop to check if the number is even or not.

```
let number = 1;

while (number <= 100) {
  if (number % 2 === 0) {
    console.log(number);
  }
  number++;
}
```

62. Write a program that prints all even numbers from 1 to 100 using a while loop without using any if statement.

```
let number = 2;

while (number <= 100) {
  console.log(number);
  number += 2;
}
```

63. Write a program that displays even numbers 1 to 50 and odd numbers 51 to 100 using a repeating loop.

```
for (let number = 1; number <= 100; number++) {
  if (number <= 50) {
    if (number % 2 === 0) {
      console.log(`Even number: ${number}`);
    }
  } else {
    if (number % 2 !== 0) {
      console.log(`Odd number: ${number}`);
    }
  }
}
```

64. Create a program that prompts the user for a number and displays the table of that number using a loop.

```
const number = parseInt(prompt("Enter a number:"));

console.log(`Multiplication table for ${number}:`);
for (let i = 1; i <= 10; i++) {
  console.log(`${number} * ${i} = ${number * i}`);
}
```

65. Create a program that displays the table of all numbers from 1 to 10.

```
for (let number = 1; number <= 10; number++) {
  console.log(`Multiplication table for ${number}:`);
  for (let i = 1; i <= 10; i++) {
    console.log(`${number} * ${i} = ${number * i}`);
  }
  console.log("\n"); // Adding a new line for clarity
between tables
}
```

66. Write a program that calculates and displays the value of the power of a number entered by the user raised to an exponent also entered by the user, using repetition loops.

```
// Prompt the user for the base number and the exponent
const baseNumber = parseFloat(prompt("Enter the base
number:"));
const exponent = parseInt(prompt("Enter the
exponent:"));

let result = 1;

// Loop to calculate the power
for (let i = 0; i < exponent; i++) {
   result *= baseNumber; // Multiply the result by the
base number 'exponent' times
}

// Display the result
console.log(`Result: ${baseNumber}^${exponent} =
${result}`);
```

67. Create a program that displays the first N first perfect squares, where N is informed by the user, using a loop.

```
// Prompt the user for the number of perfect squares to
display
const N = parseInt(prompt("Enter the number of perfect
squares to display:"));

console.log(`The first ${N} perfect squares are:`);

// Loop to find and display the first N perfect squares
for (let i = 1; i <= N; i++) {
   const perfectSquare = i * i; // Calculate the perfect
square
```

```
    console.log(perfectSquare);
  }
```

68. Write a program that asks the user for a number N and says whether it is prime or not.

```javascript
// Prompt the user for a number
const N = parseInt(prompt("Enter a number:"));

let isPrime = true;

// Check if the number is prime
if (N <= 1) {
  isPrime = false;
} else {
  for (let i = 2; i <= Math.sqrt(N); i++) {
    if (N % i === 0) {
      isPrime = false;
      break;
    }
  }
}

// Display the result
if (isPrime) {
  console.log(`${N} is a prime number.`);
} else {
  console.log(`${N} is not a prime number.`);
}
```

69. Write a program that prompts the user for a number N and displays all prime numbers less than N.

```javascript
// Prompt the user for a number
const N = parseInt(prompt("Enter a number:"));

console.log(`Prime numbers less than ${N}:`);
```

```
// Loop to check and display prime numbers less than N
for (let number = 2; number < N; number++) {
  let isPrime = true;

  if (number === 2) {
    console.log(number);
    continue;
  }

  for (let i = 2; i <= Math.sqrt(number); i++) {
    if (number % i === 0) {
      isPrime = false;
      break;
    }
  }

  if (isPrime) {
    console.log(number);
  }
}
```

70. Create a program that displays the first N prime numbers, where N is informed by the user, using a loop.

```
// Prompt the user for the number of prime numbers to
display
const N = parseInt(prompt("Enter the number of prime
numbers to display:"));

console.log(`The first ${N} prime numbers are:`);

let count = 0;
let number = 2; // Start checking from 2

// Loop to find and display the first N prime numbers
while (count < N) {
```

```
  let isPrime = true;

  for (let i = 2; i <= Math.sqrt(number); i++) {
    if (number % i === 0) {
      isPrime = false;
      break;
    }
  }

  if (isPrime) {
    console.log(number);
    count++;
  }

  number++;
}
```

71. Write a program that prompts the user for two numbers A and B and displays all numbers between A and B.

```
// Prompt the user for two numbers A and B
const A = parseInt(prompt("Enter number A:"));
const B = parseInt(prompt("Enter number B:"));

console.log(`Numbers between ${A} and ${B}:`);

// Display numbers between A and B
if (A < B) {
  for (let i = A + 1; i < B; i++) {
    console.log(i);
  }
} else {
  for (let i = B + 1; i < A; i++) {
    console.log(i);
  }
}
```

72. Write a program that reads numbers from the user until a negative number is entered, and prints the sum of the positive numbers.

```
let sum = 0;
let number = parseInt(prompt("Enter a number (enter a
negative number to stop):"));

while (number >= 0) {
  sum += number;
  number = parseInt(prompt("Enter a number (enter a
negative number to stop):"));
}

console.log(`The sum of the positive numbers entered
is: ${sum}`);
```

73. Write a program that asks the user for a number N and displays the sum of all numbers from 1 to N.

```
// Prompt the user for a number N
const N = parseInt(prompt("Enter a number:"));

let sum = 0;

// Calculate the sum of numbers from 1 to N
for (let i = 1; i <= N; i++) {
  sum += i;
}

console.log(`The sum of numbers from 1 to ${N} is:
${sum}`);
```

74. Write a program that calculates and displays the sum of even numbers from 1 to 100 using a repeating loop.

```
let sum = 0;
```

```
let number = 2; // Starting from 2 as the first even
number

while (number <= 100) {
  sum += number; // Add the current even number to the
sum
  number += 2; // Move to the next even number
}

console.log(`The sum of even numbers from 1 to 100 is:
${sum}`);
```

75. Write a program that prompts the user for a number and displays the Fibonacci sequence up to the given number using a repeating loop.

```
const limit = parseInt(prompt("Enter a number to
generate the Fibonacci sequence:"));

let a = 0, b = 1;
let result = '';

while (a <= limit) {
  result += a + ' ';
  const temp = a + b;
  a = b;
  b = temp;
}

console.log(`Fibonacci sequence up to ${limit}:
${result}`);
```

76. Write a program that reads numbers from the user until zero is entered, and displays the average of the numbers entered.

```
let sum = 0;
```

```javascript
let count = 0;
let number = parseInt(prompt("Enter a number (enter 0
to stop):"));

while (number !== 0) {
  sum += number;
  count++;
  number = parseInt(prompt("Enter a number (enter 0 to
stop):"));
}

if (count === 0) {
  console.log("No numbers were entered.");
} else {
  const average = sum / count;
  console.log(`The average of the numbers entered is:
${average}`);
}
```

77. Write a program that prompts the user for a list of numbers, until the user types the number zero, and displays the largest and smallest numbers in the list.

```javascript
let largest = Number.MIN_VALUE;
let smallest = Number.MAX_VALUE;

let number = parseInt(prompt("Enter a number (enter 0
to stop):"));

while (number !== 0) {
  if (number > largest) {
    largest = number;
  }
  if (number < smallest) {
    smallest = number;
  }
  number = parseInt(prompt("Enter a number (enter 0 to
stop):"));
```

```
}

if (largest === Number.MIN_VALUE && smallest ===
Number.MAX_VALUE) {
  console.log("No numbers were entered.");
} else {
  console.log(`The largest number entered is:
${largest}`);
  console.log(`The smallest number entered is:
${smallest}`);
}
```

78. Write a program that prompts the user for a number and displays its divisors.

```
const number = parseInt(prompt("Enter a number:"));

console.log(`The divisors of ${number} are:`);

for (let i = 1; i <= number; i++) {
  if (number % i === 0) {
    console.log(i);
  }
}
```

79. Write a program that determines the greatest common divisor (GCD) between two numbers entered by the user.

```
const num1 = parseInt(prompt("Enter the first
number:"));
const num2 = parseInt(prompt("Enter the second
number:"));

let a = num1;
let b = num2;
```

```javascript
while (b !== 0) {
  const temp = b;
  b = a % b;
  a = temp;
}

const gcd = a;

console.log(`The greatest common divisor (GCD) of
${num1} and ${num2} is: ${gcd}`);
```

80. Write a program that determines the lowest common multiple (LCM) between two numbers entered by the user.

```javascript
const num1 = parseInt(prompt("Enter the first
number:"));
const num2 = parseInt(prompt("Enter the second
number:"));

let lcm;
let larger = (num1 > num2) ? num1 : num2;

while (true) {
  if (larger % num1 === 0 && larger % num2 === 0) {
    lcm = larger;
    break;
  }
  larger++;
}

console.log(`The lowest common multiple (LCM) of
${num1} and ${num2} is: ${lcm}`);
```

81. Write a program that calculates the series below up to the tenth element:

$$e^x = 1 + x + \frac{x^2}{2!} + \frac{x^3}{3!} + \frac{x^4}{4!} + \cdots$$

```
const x = parseFloat(prompt("Enter the value of x:"));

let result = 1;
let factorial = 1;

for (let i = 1; i <= 10; i++) {
  factorial *= i;
  result += Math.pow(x, i) / factorial;
}

console.log(`e^${x} up to the tenth element is
approximately: ${result}`);
```

82. Rewrite the previous exercise code until the difference between the terms is less than 0.001.

```
const x = parseFloat(prompt("Enter the value of x:"));

let result = 1;
let term = 1;
let factorial = 1;
let i = 1;

while (Math.abs(term) >= 0.001) {
  factorial *= i;
  term = Math.pow(x, i) / factorial;
  result += term;
  i++;
}

console.log(`e^${x} with a difference less than 0.001
```

is approximately: ${result}`);

83. Make a program that calculates the value of sine using the Taylor series according to the equation below until the difference between the terms is less than 0.001.

$$sen(x) = x - \frac{x^3}{3!} + \frac{x^5}{5!} - \frac{x^7}{7!} + \cdots$$

```
const x = parseFloat(prompt("Enter the value of x in
radians:"));

let result = 0;
let term = x;
let sign = -1;
let factorial = 1;
let i = 3;

while (Math.abs(term) >= 0.001) {
  result += term;
  sign *= -1;
  factorial *= (i - 1) * i;
  term = Math.pow(x, i) / factorial * sign;
  i += 2;
}

console.log(`The sine of ${x} is approximately:
${result}` );
```

84. Make a program that calculates the value of cosine using the Taylor series according to the equation below until the difference between the terms is less than 0.001.

$$cos(x) = 1 - \frac{x^2}{2!} + \frac{x^4}{4!} - \frac{x^6}{6!} + \frac{x^8}{8!} - \frac{x^{10}}{10!} \cdots$$

```
const x = parseFloat(prompt("Enter the value of x in
radians:"));

let result = 1;
let term = 1;
let sign = -1;
let factorial = 1;
let i = 2;

while (Math.abs(term) >= 0.001) {
  factorial *= i * (i - 1);
  term = Math.pow(x, i) / factorial * sign;
  result += term;
  sign *= -1;
  i += 2;
}

console.log(`The cosine of ${x} is approximately:
${result}`);
```

85. Write a program that displays the sine and cosine value of all numbers from 0 to 6.3, with a step of 0.1, using Taylor series to calculate the respective sines and cosines.

```
const step = 0.1;
const limit = 6.3;

for (let x = 0; x <= limit; x += step) {
  let sineResult = 0;
  let sineTerm = x;
```

```
    let sineSign = -1;
    let sineFactorial = 1;
    let sineI = 3;

    while (Math.abs(sineTerm) >= 0.001) {
        sineResult += sineTerm;
        sineSign *= -1;
        sineFactorial *= (sineI - 1) * sineI;
        sineTerm = Math.pow(x, sineI) / sineFactorial *
sineSign;
        sineI += 2;
    }

    let cosResult = 1;
    let cosTerm = 1;
    let cosSign = -1;
    let cosFactorial = 1;
    let cosI = 2;

    while (Math.abs(cosTerm) >= 0.001) {
        cosFactorial *= cosI * (cosI - 1);
        cosTerm = Math.pow(x, cosI) / cosFactorial *
cosSign;
        cosResult += cosTerm;
        cosSign *= -1;
        cosI += 2;
    }

    console.log(`x: ${x.toFixed(1)}, sin(x):
${sineResult.toFixed(4)}, cos(x):
${cosResult.toFixed(4)}`);
}
```

Arrays

86. Write a program that reads an array of integers and displays the elements in reverse order.

```
// Read the array of integers from the user
const input = prompt("Enter a list of integers
separated by spaces:");
const integers = input.split(" ").map(Number);

// Display the elements in reverse order
console.log("Elements in reverse order:");
for (let i = integers.length - 1; i >= 0; i--) {
  console.log(integers[i]);
}
```

87. Create a program that reads an array of integers and displays the sum of all the elements.

```
// Read the array of integers from the user
const input = prompt("Enter a list of integers
separated by spaces:");
const integers = input.split(" ").map(Number);

// Calculate the sum of elements in the array
let sum = 0;
for (let i = 0; i < integers.length; i++) {
  sum += integers[i];
}

console.log(`The sum of all elements is: ${sum}`);
```

88. Write a program that reads an array of integers and displays the average of the elements.

```
// Read the array of integers from the user
```

```javascript
const input = prompt("Enter a list of integers
separated by spaces:");
const integers = input.split(" ").map(Number);

// Calculate the average of elements in the array
let sum = 0;
for (let i = 0; i < integers.length; i++) {
  sum += integers[i];
}

const average = sum / integers.length;
console.log(`The average of all elements is:
${average}`);
```

89. Write a program that reads an array of integers and displays the largest element in the array.

```javascript
// Read the array of integers from the user
const input = prompt("Enter a list of integers
separated by spaces:");
const integers = input.split(" ").map(Number);

// Find the largest element in the array
let largest = integers[0];
for (let i = 1; i < integers.length; i++) {
  if (integers[i] > largest) {
    largest = integers[i];
  }
}

console.log(`The largest element in the array is:
${largest}`);
```

90. Create a program that reads two vectors of integers of the same size and displays a new vector with the sum of the corresponding elements of the two vectors.

```javascript
// Read the first vector of integers from the user
const input1 = prompt("Enter the first vector of
integers separated by spaces:");
const vector1 = input1.split(" ").map(Number);

// Read the second vector of integers from the user
const input2 = prompt("Enter the second vector of
integers separated by spaces:");
const vector2 = input2.split(" ").map(Number);

// Check if both vectors have the same length
if (vector1.length !== vector2.length) {
  console.log("Vectors should have the same size.");
} else {
  // Create a new vector with the sum of corresponding
elements
  const sumVector = [];
  for (let i = 0; i < vector1.length; i++) {
    sumVector.push(vector1[i] + vector2[i]);
  }

  console.log("The new vector with the sum of
corresponding elements:");
  console.log(sumVector);
}
```

91. Write a program that reads two arrays of integers with the same size and displays a new array with the elements resulting from the multiplication of the corresponding elements of the two arrays.

```javascript
// Read the first array of integers from the user
const input1 = prompt("Enter the first array of
integers separated by spaces:");
```

```
const array1 = input1.split(" ").map(Number);

// Read the second array of integers from the user
const input2 = prompt("Enter the second array of
integers separated by spaces:");
const array2 = input2.split(" ").map(Number);

// Check if both arrays have the same length
if (array1.length !== array2.length) {
  console.log("Arrays should have the same size.");
} else {
  // Create a new array with the multiplication of
corresponding elements
  const productArray = [];
  for (let i = 0; i < array1.length; i++) {
    productArray.push(array1[i] * array2[i]);
  }

  console.log("The new array with the product of
corresponding elements:");
  console.log(productArray);
}
```

92. Write a program that reads an array of integers and displays how many times a specific number appears in the array.

```
// Read the array of integers from the user
const input = prompt("Enter a list of integers
separated by spaces:");
const integers = input.split(" ").map(Number);

// Read the specific number to count occurrences
const numberToFind = parseInt(prompt("Enter the number
to find:"));

// Count occurrences of the specific number in the
array
```

```
let count = 0;
for (let i = 0; i < integers.length; i++) {
  if (integers[i] === numberToFind) {
    count++;
  }
}


console.log(`The number ${numberToFind} appears
${count} time(s) in the array.`);
```

93. Write a program that reads an array of integers and checks if they are in ascending order.

```
// Read the array of integers from the user
const input = prompt("Enter a list of integers
separated by spaces:");
const integers = input.split(" ").map(Number);

// Function to check if the array is in ascending order
function isAscending(arr) {
  for (let i = 1; i < arr.length; i++) {
    if (arr[i] < arr[i - 1]) {
      return false;
    }
  }
  return true;
}


// Check if the array is in ascending order and display
the result
if (isAscending(integers)) {
  console.log("The array is in ascending order.");
} else {
  console.log("The array is not in ascending order.");
}
```

94. Create a program that reads an array of integers and finds the second largest element in the array.

```
// Read the array of integers from the user
const input = prompt("Enter a list of integers
separated by spaces:");
const integers = input.split(" ").map(Number);

// Find the second largest element in the array
let firstMax = -Infinity;
let secondMax = -Infinity;

for (let i = 0; i < integers.length; i++) {
  if (integers[i] > firstMax) {
    secondMax = firstMax;
    firstMax = integers[i];
  } else if (integers[i] > secondMax && integers[i] !==
firstMax) {
    secondMax = integers[i];
  }
}

// Check if a second largest element exists
if (secondMax !== -Infinity) {
  console.log(`The second largest element in the array
is: ${secondMax}`);
} else {
  console.log("There is no second largest element in
the array.");
}
```

95. Given an array, find the kth largest and smallest element in it.

```
const input = prompt("Enter a list of integers
separated by spaces:");
const integers = input.split(" ").map(Number);
```

```javascript
const k = parseInt(prompt("Enter the value of k:"));

// Sort the array in ascending order
integers.sort((a, b) => a - b);

// Find the kth smallest and largest elements
const kthSmallest = integers[k - 1];
const kthLargest = integers[integers.length - k];

console.log(`The ${k}th smallest element in the array
is: ${kthSmallest}`);
console.log(`The ${k}th largest element in the array
is: ${kthLargest}`);
```

Solution 2

```javascript
const input = prompt("Enter a list of integers
separated by spaces:");
const integers = input.split(" ").map(Number);

const k = parseInt(prompt("Enter the value of k:"));

// Function to find kth smallest element using
quickselect algorithm
function kthSmallest(arr, k) {
  const swap = (a, b) => {
    const temp = arr[a];
    arr[a] = arr[b];
    arr[b] = temp;
  };

  const partition = (left, right, pivotIndex) => {
    const pivot = arr[pivotIndex];
    let i = left;

    swap(pivotIndex, right);
    for (let j = left; j < right; j++) {
      if (arr[j] < pivot) {
```

```javascript
        swap(i, j);
        i++;
      }
    }
    swap(i, right);
    return i;
  };

  const quickSelect = (left, right, kth) => {
    if (left === right) return arr[left];

    const pivotIndex = Math.floor(Math.random() *
(right - left + 1)) + left;
    const partitionIndex = partition(left, right,
pivotIndex);

    if (kth === partitionIndex) {
      return arr[kth];
    } else if (kth < partitionIndex) {
      return quickSelect(left, partitionIndex - 1,
kth);
    } else {
      return quickSelect(partitionIndex + 1, right,
kth);
    }
  };

  return quickSelect(0, arr.length - 1, k - 1);
}

// Find kth smallest and largest elements
const kthSmallestElement = kthSmallest([...integers],
k);
const kthLargestElement = kthSmallest([...integers],
integers.length - k + 1);

console.log(`The ${k}th smallest element in the array
is: ${kthSmallestElement}`);
```

```
console.log(`The ${k}th largest element in the array
is: ${kthLargestElement}`);
```

96. Write a program that checks if an array contains duplicate elements.

```
const input = prompt("Enter a list of integers
separated by spaces:");
const integers = input.split(" ").map(Number);

let containsDuplicate = false;

// Check for duplicate elements in the array
for (let i = 0; i < integers.length; i++) {
  for (let j = i + 1; j < integers.length; j++) {
    if (integers[i] === integers[j]) {
      containsDuplicate = true;
      break;
    }
  }
  if (containsDuplicate) {
    break;
  }
}

// Display the result
if (containsDuplicate) {
  console.log("The array contains duplicate
elements.");
} else {
  console.log("The array does not contain duplicate
elements.");
}
```

97. Given an array of size n, find an element that appears more than n/2 times. (This element is called the majority element.)

```javascript
const input = prompt("Enter a list of integers
separated by spaces:");
const integers = input.split(" ").map(Number);

let candidate = null;
let count = 0;

// Find a candidate for majority element
for (let i = 0; i < integers.length; i++) {
  if (count === 0) {
    candidate = integers[i];
    count++;
  } else {
    if (candidate === integers[i]) {
      count++;
    } else {
      count--;
    }
  }
}

// Validate if the candidate is the majority element
count = 0;
for (let i = 0; i < integers.length; i++) {
  if (integers[i] === candidate) {
    count++;
  }
}

// Display the majority element if it exists
if (count > integers.length / 2) {
  console.log(`The majority element is: ${candidate}`);
} else {
  console.log("No majority element found.");
}
```

98. Create a program that reads an array of integers and checks if all elements are even.

```
const input = prompt("Enter a list of integers
separated by spaces:");
const integers = input.split(" ").map(Number);

let allEven = true;

// Check if all elements are even
for (let i = 0; i < integers.length; i++) {
  if (integers[i] % 2 !== 0) {
    allEven = false;
    break;
  }
}

// Display the result
if (allEven) {
  console.log("All elements in the array are even.");
} else {
  console.log("Not all elements in the array are
even.");
}
```

99. Write a program that checks if an array contains triplicate elements.

```
const input = prompt("Enter a list of integers
separated by spaces:");
const integers = input.split(" ").map(Number);

let containsTriplicate = false;
const frequency = {};

// Count the frequency of each element in the array
for (let i = 0; i < integers.length; i++) {
  if (frequency[integers[i]]) {
```

```
      frequency[integers[i]]++;
    } else {
      frequency[integers[i]] = 1;
    }
  }

  // Check if any element appears three times
  for (const key in frequency) {
    if (frequency[key] >= 3) {
      containsTriplicate = true;
      break;
    }
  }

  // Display the result
  if (containsTriplicate) {
    console.log("The array contains triplicate
  elements.");
  } else {
    console.log("The array does not contain triplicate
  elements.");
  }
```

100. Given an array of random numbers, push all the zero's of the array to the end without changing the order of non-zero elements.

```
const input = prompt("Enter a list of integers
separated by spaces:");
const nums = input.split(" ").map(Number);

let nonZeroIndex = 0;

// Move non-zero elements to the front of the array
for (let i = 0; i < nums.length; i++) {
  if (nums[i] !== 0) {
    nums[nonZeroIndex] = nums[i];
    nonZeroIndex++;
```

```
    }
}

// Fill the remaining elements with zeros
while (nonZeroIndex < nums.length) {
  nums[nonZeroIndex] = 0;
  nonZeroIndex++;
}

// Display the modified array
console.log("Array after pushing zeros to the end:",
nums);
```

101. Given an unsorted array of integers, find the length of the longest consecutive elements sequence.

```
const input = prompt("Enter a list of integers
separated by spaces:");
const nums = input.split(" ").map(Number);

if (nums.length === 0) {
  console.log("Length of the longest consecutive
sequence: 0");
} else {
  const numSet = new Set(nums);
  let longestSequence = 0;

  for (const num of numSet) {
    if (!numSet.has(num - 1)) {
      let currentNum = num;
      let currentSequence = 1;

      while (numSet.has(currentNum + 1)) {
        currentNum++;
        currentSequence++;
      }

      longestSequence = Math.max(longestSequence,
```

```
currentSequence);
    }
  }

  console.log("Length of the longest consecutive
sequence:", longestSequence);
}
```

102. Given an array of integers, find all pairs in the array that sum up to a specified value.

```
const input = prompt("Enter a list of integers
separated by spaces:");
const nums = input.split(" ").map(Number);
const targetSum = Number(prompt("Enter the target
sum:"));

if (nums.length < 2) {
  console.log("Array should have at least two
elements.");
} else {
  const pairs = [];

  for (let i = 0; i < nums.length; i++) {
    for (let j = i + 1; j < nums.length; j++) {
      if (nums[i] + nums[j] === targetSum) {
        pairs.push([nums[i], nums[j]]);
      }
    }
  }

  if (pairs.length === 0) {
    console.log("No pairs found with the target sum.");
  } else {
    console.log(`Pairs with the target sum
${targetSum}:`);
    pairs.forEach(pair => console.log(pair));
  }
```

```
}
```

103. Make an algorithm that reads an array of n positions, and then creates a new vector that calculates the difference of each element with the next element.

```javascript
const input = prompt("Enter a list of integers
separated by spaces:");
const nums = input.split(" ").map(Number);

if (nums.length < 2) {
  console.log("Array should have at least two
elements.");
} else {
  const differences = [];

  for (let i = 0; i < nums.length - 1; i++) {
    differences.push(nums[i + 1] - nums[i]);
  }

  console.log("Differences between each element and the
next:");
  console.log(differences);
}
```

104. Given an array of integers, find the subarray of given length with the least average.

```javascript
const input = prompt("Enter a list of integers
separated by spaces:");
const nums = input.split(" ").map(Number);
const subarrayLength = Number(prompt("Enter the length
of the subarray:"));

if (nums.length < subarrayLength || subarrayLength <=
0) {
  console.log("Invalid input.");
```

```javascript
  } else {
    let minAvg = Infinity;
    let minIndex = 0;

    // Calculate sum for the first subarray of length
subarrayLength
    let sum = 0;
    for (let i = 0; i < subarrayLength; i++) {
      sum += nums[i];
    }

    // Find the subarray with the least average
    for (let i = subarrayLength; i < nums.length; i++) {
      sum += nums[i] - nums[i - subarrayLength];
      const avg = sum / subarrayLength;

      if (avg < minAvg) {
        minAvg = avg;
        minIndex = i - subarrayLength + 1;
      }
    }

    console.log(`Subarray with the least average
(${minAvg}):`);
    console.log(nums.slice(minIndex, minIndex +
subarrayLength));
  }
```

105. Given two sorted arrays, merge them into a single sorted array.

```javascript
const input1 = prompt("Enter sorted array 1 (integers
separated by spaces):");
const input2 = prompt("Enter sorted array 2 (integers
separated by spaces):");

const arr1 = input1.split(" ").map(Number);
const arr2 = input2.split(" ").map(Number);
```

```javascript
let i = 0,
  j = 0;
const mergedArray = [];

// Merge the two sorted arrays
while (i < arr1.length && j < arr2.length) {
  if (arr1[i] < arr2[j]) {
    mergedArray.push(arr1[i]);
    i++;
  } else {
    mergedArray.push(arr2[j]);
    j++;
  }
}

// Add remaining elements from the first array
while (i < arr1.length) {
  mergedArray.push(arr1[i]);
  i++;
}

// Add remaining elements from the second array
while (j < arr2.length) {
  mergedArray.push(arr2[j]);
  j++;
}

console.log("Merged sorted array:", mergedArray);
```

Strings

106. Create a program that reads two words and concatenates them, displaying the resulting word.

```
const word1 = prompt("Enter the first word:");
const word2 = prompt("Enter the second word:");

const concatenatedWord = word1 + word2;

console.log("Concatenated word:", concatenatedWord);
```

107. Write a program that takes a word and displays each letter separately.

```
const word = prompt("Enter a word:");
const letters = word.split('');

console.log("Letters separated:");
for (const letter of letters) {
  console.log(letter);
}
```

108. Create a program that takes a sentence and replaces all the letters "a" with "e".

```
const sentence = prompt("Enter a sentence:");
let replacedSentence = '';

for (let i = 0; i < sentence.length; i++) {
  if (sentence[i] === 'a') {
    replacedSentence += 'e';
  } else {
    replacedSentence += sentence[i];
  }
}
```

```
console.log("Modified sentence:", replacedSentence);
```

109. Create a program that takes a sentence and replaces all spaces with a new line.

```
const sentence = prompt("Enter a sentence:");
const replacedSentence = sentence.split('
').join('\n');

console.log("Modified sentence:");
console.log(replacedSentence);
```

110. Write a program that receives a name and checks that it starts with the letter "A".

```
const name = prompt("Enter a name:");

if (name.charAt(0).toUpperCase() === 'A') {
  console.log(`${name} starts with the letter A.`);
} else {
  console.log(`${name} does not start with the letter
A.`);
}
```

111. Write a program that reads a word and checks if it is a palindrome (if it can be read backwards the same way).

```
const word = prompt("Enter a word:");
const reversedWord = word.split('').reverse().join('');

if (word === reversedWord) {
  console.log(`${word} is a palindrome.`);
} else {
  console.log(`${word} is not a palindrome.`);
}
```

112. Create a program that reads two words and checks if the second word is an anagram of the first.

```javascript
const word1 = prompt("Enter the first word:");
const word2 = prompt("Enter the second word:");

const sortedWord1 =
word1.toLowerCase().split('').sort().join('');
const sortedWord2 =
word2.toLowerCase().split('').sort().join('');

if (sortedWord1 === sortedWord2) {
  console.log(`${word2} is an anagram of ${word1}.`);
} else {
  console.log(`${word2} is not an anagram of
${word1}.`);
}
```

113. Write a program that takes a full name and displays only the first name.

```javascript
const fullName = prompt("Enter your full name:");
const firstName = fullName.split(' ')[0];

console.log("First name:", firstName);
```

114. Make a program that receives a sentence and displays the amount of blank spaces present in it.

```javascript
const sentence = prompt("Enter a sentence:");
let spaceCount = 0;

for (let i = 0; i < sentence.length; i++) {
  if (sentence.charAt(i) === ' ') {
    spaceCount++;
  }
}
```

```
console.log("Number of blank spaces:", spaceCount);
```

115. Create a program that reads a word and displays the number of vowels present in it.

```
const word = prompt("Enter a word:");
const vowels = ['a', 'e', 'i', 'o', 'u'];
let vowelCount = 0;

for (let i = 0; i < word.length; i++) {
  if (vowels.includes(word.charAt(i).toLowerCase())) {
    vowelCount++;
  }
}

console.log("Number of vowels:", vowelCount);
```

116. Create a program that reads a word and displays the number of vowels and consonants present in it.

```
const word = prompt("Enter a word:");
const vowels = ['a', 'e', 'i', 'o', 'u'];
let vowelCount = 0;
let consonantCount = 0;

for (let i = 0; i < word.length; i++) {
  const currentChar = word.charAt(i).toLowerCase();
  if (vowels.includes(currentChar)) {
    vowelCount++;
  } else if (currentChar >= 'a' && currentChar <= 'z')
{
    consonantCount++;
  }
}

console.log("Number of vowels:", vowelCount);
console.log("Number of consonants:", consonantCount);
```

117. Write a program that takes a full name and displays the last name (last name) first.

```
const fullName = prompt("Enter your full name:");
const namesArray = fullName.split(' ');
const lastName = namesArray[namesArray.length - 1];

console.log("Last name first:", lastName);
```

118. Implement a method to perform basic string compression using the counts of repeated characters. For instance, the string aabcccccaaa would become a2b1c5a3.

```
const str = "aabcccccaaa";
let compressedString = '';
let count = 1;

for (let i = 0; i < str.length; i++) {
  if (str[i] === str[i + 1]) {
    count++;
  } else {
    compressedString += str[i] + count;
    count = 1;
  }
}

console.log("Compressed string:", compressedString);
```

119. Rawwords: Write an algorithm that checks whether a word is a "rawword". A word is considered a "prime word" if the sum of the letter values (where 'a' = 1, 'b' = 2, etc.) is a prime number.

```
function isPrime(n) {
  if (n <= 1) {
    return false;
  }
```

```javascript
  for (let i = 2; i <= Math.sqrt(n); i++) {
    if (n % i === 0) {
      return false;
    }
  }
  return true;
}

function calculateLetterValue(char) {
  return char.toLowerCase().charCodeAt(0) - 96; // 'a'
= 1, 'b' = 2, ...
}

function isRawWord(word) {
  let sum = 0;
  for (let i = 0; i < word.length; i++) {
    sum += calculateLetterValue(word[i]);
  }
  return isPrime(sum);
}

const inputWord = prompt("Enter a word:");
if (isRawWord(inputWord)) {
  console.log(`"${inputWord}" is a rawword.`);
} else {
  console.log(`"${inputWord}" is not a rawword.`);
}
```

120. Given a list of strings, write a function to determine the longest common prefix.

```javascript
function longestCommonPrefix(strs) {
  if (strs.length === 0) {
    return "";
  }

  let prefix = strs[0];
  for (let i = 1; i < strs.length; i++) {
```

```javascript
    let j = 0;
    while (j < prefix.length && j < strs[i].length &&
prefix.charAt(j) === strs[i].charAt(j)) {
      j++;
    }
    prefix = prefix.slice(0, j);
    if (prefix === "") {
      return "";
    }
  }
  return prefix;
}

// Example usage:
const strings = ["flower", "flow", "flight"];
const commonPrefix = longestCommonPrefix(strings);
console.log("Longest common prefix:", commonPrefix);
```

Matrices

121. Write a program that fills a 3x3 matrix with values entered by the user and displays the sum of the main diagonal values.

```
const matrix = [];
let sum = 0;

// Prompt user for matrix values
for (let i = 0; i < 3; i++) {
  matrix[i] = [];
  for (let j = 0; j < 3; j++) {
    matrix[i][j] = parseInt(prompt(`Enter value for
matrix[${i}][${j}]:`));
    if (i === j) {
      sum += matrix[i][j]; // Add values on the main
diagonal
    }
  }
}

// Display matrix and sum of main diagonal
console.log("Matrix:", matrix);
console.log("Sum of main diagonal values:", sum);
```

122. Write a program that fills a 4x4 matrix with random values and displays the transposed matrix.

```
const matrix = [];
const transposedMatrix = [];

// Fill matrix with random values
for (let i = 0; i < 4; i++) {
  matrix[i] = [];
  for (let j = 0; j < 4; j++) {
    matrix[i][j] = Math.floor(Math.random() * 10); //
```

```
Random values from 0 to 9
  }
}

// Display original matrix
console.log("Original Matrix:");
console.log(matrix);

// Transpose the matrix
for (let i = 0; i < 4; i++) {
  transposedMatrix[i] = [];
  for (let j = 0; j < 4; j++) {
    transposedMatrix[i][j] = matrix[j][i];
  }
}

// Display transposed matrix
console.log("\nTransposed Matrix:");
console.log(transposedMatrix);
```

123. Write a program that fills a 5x5 matrix with integers and displays the largest value in the matrix and its position.

```
const matrix = [];
let largestValue = -Infinity;
let largestValueRow = -1;
let largestValueCol = -1;

// Fill matrix with random integers
for (let i = 0; i < 5; i++) {
  matrix[i] = [];
  for (let j = 0; j < 5; j++) {
    matrix[i][j] = Math.floor(Math.random() * 100); //
Random integers between 0 and 99
    if (matrix[i][j] > largestValue) {
      largestValue = matrix[i][j];
      largestValueRow = i;
```

```
      largestValueCol = j;
    }
  }
}

// Display original matrix
console.log("Matrix:");
console.log(matrix);

// Display largest value and its position
console.log(`Largest value: ${largestValue} at position
[${largestValueRow}][${largestValueCol}]`);
```

124. Count negative numbers in a matrix

```
const matrix = [
  [2, -3, 5, 0],
  [-7, 8, -1, 4],
  [6, 0, -9, 10],
  [-12, -15, 17, 20]
];

let negativeCount = 0;

// Count negative numbers in the matrix
for (let i = 0; i < matrix.length; i++) {
  for (let j = 0; j < matrix[i].length; j++) {
    if (matrix[i][j] < 0) {
      negativeCount++;
    }
  }
}

console.log("Number of negative numbers in the
matrix:", negativeCount);
```

125. Write a program that reads a 3x3 matrix and calculates the average of the values present in the even positions (sum of the even indices) of the matrix.

```javascript
const matrix = [];
let sum = 0;
let count = 0;

// Fill matrix with user input
for (let i = 0; i < 3; i++) {
  matrix[i] = [];
  for (let j = 0; j < 3; j++) {
    matrix[i][j] = parseInt(prompt(`Enter value for
matrix[${i}][${j}]:`));
    if ((i + j) % 2 === 0) {
      sum += matrix[i][j];
      count++;
    }
  }
}

// Calculate average of values at even positions
const average = count !== 0 ? sum / count : 0;

console.log("Matrix:", matrix);
console.log("Average of values at even positions:",
average);
```

126. Calculate the sum of boundary elements of a matrix.

```javascript
const matrix = [
  [1, 2, 3],
  [4, 5, 6],
  [7, 8, 9]
];

let sum = 0;
```

```javascript
// Calculate sum of boundary elements
for (let i = 0; i < matrix.length; i++) {
  for (let j = 0; j < matrix[i].length; j++) {
    if (i === 0 || i === matrix.length - 1 || j === 0
|| j === matrix[i].length - 1) {
      sum += matrix[i][j];
    }
  }
}

console.log("Matrix:", matrix);
console.log("Sum of boundary elements:", sum);
```

127. Write a program that reads a 4x4 matrix and checks if it is a diagonal matrix, that is, if all elements outside the main diagonal are equal to zero.

```javascript
const matrix = [
  [5, 0, 0, 0],
  [0, 8, 0, 0],
  [0, 0, 3, 0],
  [0, 0, 0, 2]
];

let isDiagonal = true;

// Check if it's a diagonal matrix
for (let i = 0; i < matrix.length; i++) {
  for (let j = 0; j < matrix[i].length; j++) {
    if (i !== j && matrix[i][j] !== 0) {
      isDiagonal = false;
      break;
    }
  }
}

console.log("Matrix:", matrix);
```

```javascript
if (isDiagonal) {
  console.log("It is a diagonal matrix.");
} else {
  console.log("It is not a diagonal matrix.");
}
```

128. Write a program to determine whether a given matrix is symmetric.

```javascript
function isSymmetric(matrix) {
  const rows = matrix.length;
  const cols = matrix[0].length;

  // Check if matrix is square
  if (rows !== cols) {
    return false;
  }

  // Check if it's symmetric
  for (let i = 0; i < rows; i++) {
    for (let j = 0; j < cols; j++) {
      if (matrix[i][j] !== matrix[j][i]) {
        return false;
      }
    }
  }

  return true;
}

// Example matrix
const matrix = [
  [1, 2, 3],
  [2, 4, 5],
  [3, 5, 6]
];

console.log("Matrix:", matrix);
```

```
if (isSymmetric(matrix)) {
  console.log("The matrix is symmetric.");
} else {
  console.log("The matrix is not symmetric.");
}
```

129. Write a program that fills a 4x4 matrix with random numbers and displays the sum of the values present in each row and in each column.

```
function generateMatrix(rows, cols) {
  const matrix = [];
  for (let i = 0; i < rows; i++) {
    matrix[i] = [];
    for (let j = 0; j < cols; j++) {
      matrix[i][j] = Math.floor(Math.random() * 10); //
Random integers between 0 and 9
    }
  }
  return matrix;
}

function sumRows(matrix) {
  return matrix.map(row => row.reduce((acc, val) => acc
+ val, 0));
}

function sumColumns(matrix) {
  const cols = matrix[0].length;
  const sums = Array(cols).fill(0);

  for (let i = 0; i < cols; i++) {
    for (let j = 0; j < matrix.length; j++) {
      sums[i] += matrix[j][i];
    }
  }
  return sums;
}
```

```
const matrix = generateMatrix(4, 4);
console.log("Matrix:", matrix);

const rowSums = sumRows(matrix);
console.log("Sum of values in each row:", rowSums);

const colSums = sumColumns(matrix);
console.log("Sum of values in each column:", colSums);
```

130. Write a program that reads a 3x3 matrix and calculates the determinant of the matrix.

```
function determinant(matrix) {
  const [ [a, b, c], [d, e, f], [g, h, i] ] = matrix;
  return a * (e * i - f * h) - b * (d * i - f * g) + c
* (d * h - e * g);
}

// Example 3x3 matrix
const matrix = [
  [2, -3, 1],
  [5, 4, 7],
  [0, 8, -6]
];

console.log("Matrix:", matrix);
console.log("Determinant:", determinant(matrix));
```

131. Write a program that reads two 2x2 matrices and displays the sum of the two matrices.

```
function matrixSum(matrix1, matrix2) {
  const result = [];
  for (let i = 0; i < matrix1.length; i++) {
    result[i] = [];
    for (let j = 0; j < matrix1[i].length; j++) {
```

```
      result[i][j] = matrix1[i][j] + matrix2[i][j];
    }
  }
  return result;
}

// Example matrices
const matrix1 = [
  [2, 3],
  [4, 5]
];

const matrix2 = [
  [1, 2],
  [3, 4]
];

console.log("Matrix 1:", matrix1);
console.log("Matrix 2:", matrix2);

const resultMatrix = matrixSum(matrix1, matrix2);
console.log("Sum of the matrices:", resultMatrix);
```

132. Write a program that reads two matrices and returns the multiplication between them as an answer. The program should observe whether or not it is possible to perform the multiplication between the two matrices.

```
function matrixMultiplication(matrix1, matrix2) {
  const rows1 = matrix1.length;
  const cols1 = matrix1[0].length;
  const rows2 = matrix2.length;
  const cols2 = matrix2[0].length;

  if (cols1 !== rows2) {
    return "Matrix multiplication not possible: Invalid
dimensions";
```

```javascript
  }
  const result = [];
  for (let i = 0; i < rows1; i++) {
    result[i] = [];
    for (let j = 0; j < cols2; j++) {
      let sum = 0;
      for (let k = 0; k < cols1; k++) {
        sum += matrix1[i][k] * matrix2[k][j];
      }
      result[i][j] = sum;
    }
  }
  return result;
}

function createMatrix(rows, cols) {
  const matrix = [];
  for (let i = 0; i < rows; i++) {
    matrix[i] = [];
    for (let j = 0; j < cols; j++) {
      const value = parseInt(prompt(`Enter value for
matrix[${i}][${j}]:`));
      matrix[i][j] = isNaN(value) ? 0 : value;
    }
  }
  return matrix;
}

const rows1 = parseInt(prompt("Enter the number of rows
for matrix 1:"));
const cols1 = parseInt(prompt("Enter the number of
columns for matrix 1:"));
const rows2 = parseInt(prompt("Enter the number of rows
for matrix 2:"));
const cols2 = parseInt(prompt("Enter the number of
columns for matrix 2:"));
```

```javascript
const matrix1 = createMatrix(rows1, cols1);
const matrix2 = createMatrix(rows2, cols2);

console.log("Matrix 1:", matrix1);
console.log("Matrix 2:", matrix2);

const resultMatrix = matrixMultiplication(matrix1,
matrix2);
if (typeof resultMatrix === 'string') {
  console.log(resultMatrix);
} else {
  console.log("Result of matrix multiplication:",
resultMatrix);
}
```

133. Print a matrix in spiral order.

```javascript
function spiralOrder(matrix) {
  if (matrix.length === 0) return [];

  const result = [];
  let rowStart = 0,
    rowEnd = matrix.length - 1;
  let colStart = 0,
    colEnd = matrix[0].length - 1;

  while (rowStart <= rowEnd && colStart <= colEnd) {
    // Print top row
    for (let i = colStart; i <= colEnd; i++) {
      result.push(matrix[rowStart][i]);
    }
    rowStart++;

    // Print right column
    for (let i = rowStart; i <= rowEnd; i++) {
      result.push(matrix[i][colEnd]);
    }
    colEnd--;
```

```
    // Print bottom row (if any)
    if (rowStart <= rowEnd) {
      for (let i = colEnd; i >= colStart; i--) {
        result.push(matrix[rowEnd][i]);
      }
      rowEnd--;
    }

    // Print left column (if any)
    if (colStart <= colEnd) {
      for (let i = rowEnd; i >= rowStart; i--) {
        result.push(matrix[i][colStart]);
      }
      colStart++;
    }
  }
  return result;
}

// Example matrix
const matrix = [
  [1, 2, 3],
  [4, 5, 6],
  [7, 8, 9]
];

console.log("Spiral order:", spiralOrder(matrix));
```

134. Write a program that reads an m x n matrix, indicating the location where there are mines in a Minesweeper game (being 0 for a neutral field, and 1 for locations where there would be mines), and the program should return a matrix indicating, for each position, the number of mines in neighboring houses.

```
function minesweeper(matrix) {
  const rows = matrix.length;
```

```
  const cols = matrix[0].length;
  const result = [];

  for (let i = 0; i < rows; i++) {
    result.push([]);
    for (let j = 0; j < cols; j++) {
      let count = 0;

      for (let r = i - 1; r <= i + 1; r++) {
        for (let c = j - 1; c <= j + 1; c++) {
          if (r >= 0 && r < rows && c >= 0 && c < cols
&& !(r === i && c === j)) {
            count += matrix[r][c];
          }
        }
      }
      result[i][j] = count;
    }
  }
  return result;
}

// Example matrix with mine locations
const matrix = [
  [0, 1, 0],
  [1, 1, 1],
  [0, 1, 0]
];

console.log(minesweeper(matrix));
```

135. Make a function that receives a 3x3 matrix representing the game of tic-tac-toe, and check if there is a winner, if there is a tie, or if the game is not over yet

```
function checkTicTacToe(matrix) {
  // Check rows, columns, and diagonals for a winner
```

```
for (let i = 0; i < 3; i++) {
  if (
    matrix[i][0] !== 0 &&
    matrix[i][0] === matrix[i][1] &&
    matrix[i][0] === matrix[i][2]
  ) {
    return `Player ${matrix[i][0]} wins!`;
  }
  if (
    matrix[0][i] !== 0 &&
    matrix[0][i] === matrix[1][i] &&
    matrix[0][i] === matrix[2][i]
  ) {
    return `Player ${matrix[0][i]} wins!`;
  }
}

if (
  matrix[0][0] !== 0 &&
  matrix[0][0] === matrix[1][1] &&
  matrix[0][0] === matrix[2][2]
) {
  return `Player ${matrix[0][0]} wins!`;
}

if (
  matrix[0][2] !== 0 &&
  matrix[0][2] === matrix[1][1] &&
  matrix[0][2] === matrix[2][0]
) {
  return `Player ${matrix[0][2]} wins!`;
}

// Check for a tie or game still in progress
for (let i = 0; i < 3; i++) {
  for (let j = 0; j < 3; j++) {
    if (matrix[i][j] === 0) {
      return "Game still in progress";
```

```
      }
    }
  }
  return "It's a tie!";
}

// Example 3x3 matrix representing tic-tac-toe game
const game1 = [
  [1, 0, 1],
  [0, 1, 0],
  [1, 0, 1]
];

const game2 = [
  [1, 0, 1],
  [0, 1, 0],
  [0, 1, 0]
];

console.log(checkTicTacToe(game1)); // Player 1 wins!
console.log(checkTicTacToe(game2)); // It's a tie!
```

Recursive Functions

136. Write a recursive function to calculate the factorial of a number.

```javascript
function factorial(n) {
  if (n === 0 || n === 1) {
    return 1;
  } else {
    return n * factorial(n - 1);
  }
}


// Example usage
const number = 5;
console.log(`Factorial of ${number} is:`,
factorial(number));
```

137. Implement a recursive function to calculate the Fibonacci sequence up to a given number.

```javascript
function fibonacci(n, sequence = [0, 1]) {
  if (n === 0) {
    return [0];
  } else if (n === 1) {
    return sequence;
  } else {
    const nextNumber = sequence[sequence.length - 1] +
sequence[sequence.length - 2];
    if (nextNumber <= n) {
      sequence.push(nextNumber);
      return fibonacci(n, sequence);
    } else {
      return sequence;
    }
  }
}
```

```
// Example usage
const number = 50;
console.log("Fibonacci sequence up to", number, "is:",
fibonacci(number));
```

138. Create a recursive function to check if a number is prime.

```
function isPrime(num, divisor = 2) {
  if (num <= 2) {
    return (num === 2);
  }
  if (num % divisor === 0) {
    return (num === divisor);
  }
  if (divisor * divisor > num) {
    return true;
  }
  return isPrime(num, divisor + 1);
}
```

```
// Example usage
const number = 17;
console.log(`Is ${number} prime?`, isPrime(number)); //
Expected output: true
```

139. Develop a recursive function to calculate the sum of the digits of an integer.

```
function sumOfDigits(n) {
  if (n < 10) {
    return n;
  } else {
    return (n % 10) + sumOfDigits(Math.floor(n / 10));
  }
}
```

```
// Example usage
const number = 12345;
console.log("Sum of digits:", sumOfDigits(number)); //
Expected output: 15
```

140. Write a recursive function to calculate the power of an integer raised to an exponent.

```
function power(base, exponent) {
  if (exponent === 0) {
    return 1;
  } else {
    return base * power(base, exponent - 1);
  }
}
```

```
// Example usage
const base = 3;
const exp = 4;
console.log(`${base} raised to the power ${exp} is:`,
power(base, exp)); // Expected output: 81
```

141. Implement a recursive function to find the greatest common divisor (GCD) of two numbers.

```
function gcd(a, b) {
  if (b === 0) {
    return a;
  } else {
    return gcd(b, a % b);
  }
}
```

```
// Example usage
const num1 = 48;
const num2 = 18;
```

```javascript
console.log(`GCD of ${num1} and ${num2} is:`, gcd(num1,
num2)); // Expected output: 6
```

142. Create a recursive function to reverse a string.

```javascript
function reverseString(str) {
  if (str === "") {
    return "";
  } else {
    return reverseString(str.substr(1)) +
str.charAt(0);
  }
}
```

```javascript
// Example usage
const string = "Hello, world!";
console.log("Reversed string:", reverseString(string));
// Expected output: "!dlrow ,olleH"
```

143. Develop a recursive function to find the smallest value in an array.

```javascript
function findMin(arr) {
  if (arr.length === 1) {
    return arr[0];
  } else {
    const subMin = findMin(arr.slice(1));
    return arr[0] < subMin ? arr[0] : subMin;
  }
}
```

```javascript
// Example usage
const array = [10, 5, 8, 3, 7, 2];
console.log("The smallest value in the array is:",
findMin(array)); // Expected output: 2
```

144. Write a recursive function to determine whether a word is a palindrome.

```
function isPalindrome(word) {
  if (word.length <= 1) {
    return true;
  } else {
    if (word[0] === word[word.length - 1]) {
      return isPalindrome(word.substring(1, word.length
- 1));
    } else {
      return false;
    }
  }
}


// Example usage
const word1 = "racecar";
const word2 = "hello";
console.log(`${word1} is a palindrome:`,
isPalindrome(word1)); // Expected output: true
console.log(`${word2} is a palindrome:`,
isPalindrome(word2)); // Expected output: false
```

145. Implement a recursive function to calculate the sum of elements of an array.

```
function arraySum(arr) {
  if (arr.length === 0) {
    return 0;
  } else {
    return arr[0] + arraySum(arr.slice(1));
  }
}


// Example usage
const array = [1, 2, 3, 4, 5];
console.log("Sum of elements in the array:",
```

```
arraySum(array)); // Expected output: 15
```

Regular Expressions

146. Write a regex to validate email addresses, ensuring it contains @ and . symbols.

```
const emailPattern = /^[^\s@]+@[^\s@]+\.[^\s@]+$/;

// Example usage
const email1 = "example@example.com";
const email2 = "invalid.email";
console.log(`Email "${email1}" is valid:`,
emailPattern.test(email1));
// Expected output: true

console.log(`Email "${email2}" is valid:`,
emailPattern.test(email2));
// Expected output: false
```

147. Extract all valid dates from a string in the format YYYY-MM-DD or DD/MM/YYYY.

```
const dateString = "Some text with dates: 2023-11-21,
12/25/2024, 05/06/2022, 2021-13-45";

const datePattern =
/\b\d{4}-\d{2}-\d{2}\b|\b\d{2}\/\d{2}\/\d{4}\b/g;
const validDates = dateString.match(datePattern);

console.log("Valid dates found:", validDates);
```

148. Check if a given string is a valid credit card number (typically 16 digits, sometimes separated by - or spaces).

```
function isValidCreditCardNumber(str) {
  // Remove dashes and spaces
```

```javascript
  const cleanStr = str.replace(/-|\s/g, '');

  // Check if the string is 16 digits and contains only
numbers
  const creditCardPattern = /^\d{16}$/;

  return creditCardPattern.test(cleanStr);
}


// Example usage
const cardNumber1 = "1234-5678-9012-3456";
const cardNumber2 = "1234567890123456";
const cardNumber3 = "123456789012345"; // Invalid
length

console.log(`"${cardNumber1}" is a valid credit card
number:`, isValidCreditCardNumber(cardNumber1)); //
Expected output: true
console.log(`"${cardNumber2}" is a valid credit card
number:`, isValidCreditCardNumber(cardNumber2)); //
Expected output: true
console.log(`"${cardNumber3}" is a valid credit card
number:`, isValidCreditCardNumber(cardNumber3)); //
Expected output: false
```

149. Validate passwords to ensure they contain at least one uppercase character, one lowercase character, one digit, one special character, and are at least 8 characters long.

```javascript
function validatePassword(password) {
  const passwordPattern =
/^(?=.*[a-z])(?=.*[A-Z])(?=.*\d)(?=.*[@$!%*?&])[A-Za-z\
d@$!%*?&]{8,}$/;
  return passwordPattern.test(password);
}


// Example usage
```

```javascript
const password1 = "Passw0rd!";
const password2 = "password"; // Doesn't meet criteria

console.log(`"${password1}" is a valid password:`,
validatePassword(password1)); // Expected output: true
console.log(`"${password2}" is a valid password:`,
validatePassword(password2)); // Expected output: false
```

150. Replace multiple spaces in a text with a single space.

```javascript
const text = "This    is    a    text    with
multiple    spaces";

const newText = text.replace(/\s+/g, ' ');

console.log(newText);
```

151. Validate and extract currency values from a text (e.g., $100.25).

```javascript
const text = "The total amount is $100.25 and $50.50
for other items.";

const currencyPattern = /\$\d+(\.\d{1,2})?/g;
const currencyValues = text.match(currencyPattern);

console.log(currencyValues);
```

152. Write a regex to extract all URLs from a text.

```javascript
const text = "Visit our website at
https://www.example.com or check out
http://test.example.org/path/page.html";

const urlPattern = /https?:\/\/\S+/g;
const extractedURLs = text.match(urlPattern);
```

```
console.log(extractedURLs);
```

153. Extract all hex color codes from a text (e.g., #AABBCC or #ABC).

```
const text = "The colors #AABBCC and #123 are commonly
used in designs.";

const hexColorPattern = /#[0-9A-Fa-f]{3,6}\b/g;
const extractedColors = text.match(hexColorPattern);

console.log(extractedColors);
```

154. Extract all valid IPv4 addresses from a text.

```
const text = "The IP addresses are 192.168.0.1 and
10.0.0.1, but not 999.888.777.666 or 256.256.256.256.";

const ipv4Pattern = /\b(?:\d{1,3}\.){3}\d{1,3}\b/g;
const extractedIPs = text.match(ipv4Pattern);

console.log(extractedIPs);
```

155. Use capture groups to rearrange date formats (convert YYYY-MM-DD to DD-MM-YYYY).

```
const dateString = "2023-11-21";

const rearrangedDate =
dateString.replace(/(\d{4})-(\d{2})-(\d{2})/g,
"$3-$2-$1");

console.log(rearrangedDate); // Output: 21-11-2023
```

Sorting Algorithms

156. Implement the Bubble Sort algorithm

```
function bubbleSort(arr) {
  const n = arr.length;

  for (let i = 0; i < n - 1; i++) {
    // Flag to optimize the sorting process
    let swapped = false;

    for (let j = 0; j < n - i - 1; j++) {
      if (arr[j] > arr[j + 1]) {
        // Swap elements if they are in the wrong order
        [arr[j], arr[j + 1]] = [arr[j + 1], arr[j]];
        swapped = true;
      }
    }

    // If no two elements were swapped in the inner
loop, the array is already sorted
    if (!swapped) break;
  }

  return arr;
}

// Example usage:
const unsortedArray = [64, 25, 12, 22, 11];
const sortedArray = bubbleSort(unsortedArray);
console.log(sortedArray); // Output: [11, 12, 22, 25,
64]
```

157. Implement the Selection Sort algorithm

```
function bubbleSort(arr) {
  const n = arr.length;
```

```javascript
  for (let i = 0; i < n - 1; i++) {
    // Flag to optimize the sorting process
    let swapped = false;

    for (let j = 0; j < n - i - 1; j++) {
      if (arr[j] > arr[j + 1]) {
        // Swap elements if they are in the wrong order
        [arr[j], arr[j + 1]] = [arr[j + 1], arr[j]];
        swapped = true;
      }
    }

    // If no two elements were swapped in the inner
loop, the array is already sorted
    if (!swapped) break;
  }

  return arr;
}

// Example usage:
const unsortedArray = [64, 25, 12, 22, 11];
const sortedArray = bubbleSort(unsortedArray);
console.log(sortedArray); // Output: [11, 12, 22, 25,
64]
```

158. Implement the Insertion Sort algorithm

```javascript
function insertionSort(arr) {
  const n = arr.length;

  for (let i = 1; i < n; i++) {
    let current = arr[i];
    let j = i - 1;

    // Move elements of arr[0..i-1] that are greater
than current to one position ahead of their current
```

```
position
    while (j >= 0 && arr[j] > current) {
      arr[j + 1] = arr[j];
      j--;
    }
    arr[j + 1] = current;
  }

  return arr;
}

// Example usage:
const unsortedArray = [64, 25, 12, 22, 11];
const sortedArray = insertionSort(unsortedArray);
console.log(sortedArray); // Output: [11, 12, 22, 25, 64]
```

159. Implement the Merge Sort algorithm

```
function mergeSort(arr) {
  if (arr.length <= 1) {
    return arr;
  }

  const mid = Math.floor(arr.length / 2);
  const left = arr.slice(0, mid);
  const right = arr.slice(mid);

  return merge(mergeSort(left), mergeSort(right));
}

function merge(left, right) {
  let result = [];
  let leftIndex = 0;
  let rightIndex = 0;

  while (leftIndex < left.length && rightIndex <
right.length) {
```

```
    if (left[leftIndex] < right[rightIndex]) {
      result.push(left[leftIndex]);
      leftIndex++;
    } else {
      result.push(right[rightIndex]);
      rightIndex++;
    }
  }

  return
result.concat(left.slice(leftIndex)).concat(right.slice
(rightIndex));
}

// Example usage:
const unsortedArray = [64, 25, 12, 22, 11];
const sortedArray = mergeSort(unsortedArray);
console.log(sortedArray); // Output: [11, 12, 22, 25,
64]
```

160. Implement the Quick Sort algorithm

```
function quickSort(arr, left = 0, right = arr.length -
1) {
  if (left < right) {
    const partitionIndex = partition(arr, left, right);
    quickSort(arr, left, partitionIndex - 1);
    quickSort(arr, partitionIndex + 1, right);
  }
  return arr;
}

function partition(arr, left, right) {
  const pivot = arr[right];
  let i = left - 1;

  for (let j = left; j < right; j++) {
    if (arr[j] < pivot) {
```

```
      i++;
      swap(arr, i, j);
    }
  }

  swap(arr, i + 1, right);
  return i + 1;
}

function swap(arr, i, j) {
  const temp = arr[i];
  arr[i] = arr[j];
  arr[j] = temp;
}

// Example usage:
const unsortedArray = [64, 25, 12, 22, 11];
const sortedArray = quickSort(unsortedArray);
console.log(sortedArray); // Output: [11, 12, 22, 25,
64]
```

Complete List of Exercises

Additional Content

In case you want to access the code of all the exercises, you can get it from the link below:

https://forms.gle/cY9kuJou8JkG84NaA

Each file is named with the exercise number, with the extension .js

About the Author

Ruhan Avila da Conceição (@ruhanconceicao, on social media) holds a degree in Computer Engineering (2015) from the Federal University of Pelotas and a Master's in Computing (2016) also from the same university. Since 2018 he has been a professor at the Federal Institute of Education, Science and Technology in the field of Informatics, where he teaches, among others, the disciplines of Object Oriented Programming, Visual Programming and Mobile Device Programming.

In 2014, even as an undergraduate student, Ruhan received the title of Researcher from Rio Grande do Sul in the Young Innovator category due to his academic and scientific career during his years at the university. His research topic has always been related to the algorithmic development of efficient solutions for encoding videos in real time. Still with regard to scientific research, Ruhan accumulates dozens of works published in national and international congresses, as well as articles in scientific journals of great relevance, and two computer programs registered at the National Institute of Intellectual Property.

Initiated in programming in the C language, Ruhan Conceição has extensive knowledge in JavaScript languages, as well as their libraries and frameworks ReactJS, React Native, NextJS; and Java. In addition, the author has also developed projects in Python, C#, Matlab, GoogleScript and C++.

www.ingramcontent.com/pod-product-compliance
Lightning Source LLC
Chambersburg PA
CBHW071253050326
40690CB00011B/2378